Muhammad ﷺ
and
Islam

Steve White-Thomson

HODDER
Wayland

an imprint of Hodder Children's Books

Religious Lives

The Buddha and Buddhism
Guru Nanak and Sikhism
Jesus and Christianity

Krishna and Hinduism
Moses and Judaism
Muhammad and Islam

For more information on this series and other Hodder Wayland titles, go to
www.hodderwayland.co.uk

© White-Thomson Publishing Ltd 2006

Produced for Hodder Wayland by White-Thomson Publishing Ltd
Bridgewater Business Centre, 210 High Street, Lewes, East Sussex BN7 2NH, UK

First published in 2006 by Hodder Wayland, an imprint of Hodder Children's Books

This book is adapted from *Muhammad and Islam* (*Great Religious Leaders* series) by Kerena Marchant,
published by Hodder Wayland in 2002

British Library Cataloguing in Publication Data

Nason, Ruth
Muhammad and Islam. - Adapted Ed. - (Religious Lives)
1. Muhammad, Prophet, d. 632 - Juvenile literature 2. Islam -
Juvenile literature
I. Title II.Marchant, Kerena
297.6'3
ISBN-10: 0750247975
ISBN-13: 9780750247979

Printed in China

Hodder Children's Books
A division of Hodder Headline Limited
338 Euston Road, London NW1 3BH

Title page: Muslims in Lamu, Kenya, celebrate a festival.

Picture Acknowledgements: The publisher would like to thank the following for permission to reproduce their pictures:
Art Directors and Trip Photo Library 8, 12, 15 (top) (H Rogers), 15 (bottom) (Ibrahim), 18 (H Rogers), 24, 31 (H Rogers), 36;
Bridgeman Art Library 11, 13; Britstock-IFA title page (Peter Sanders), 4 (Beckwith/Fisher), 5 (bottom) (Hinata Haga), 28 (Peter Sanders), 29 (Kazuyoshi Nomachi), 30 (top) (Kazuyoshi Nomachi), 30 (bottom) (Peter Sanders), 32 (Peter Sanders), 34, 35 (Peter Sanders), 37 (Peter Sanders), 38 (Kazuyoshi Nomachi); Eye Ubiquitous 41 (Bennett Dean), 43 (Julia Waterlow); Impact 6 (David S. Silverberg), 7 (John Cole), 40 (Mark Henley); Peter Sanders cover top, cover main, 5 (top), 14, 19, 20, 21, 22, 23, 25, 27, 33 (top), 33 (bottom), 39 (bottom), 42, 44, 45; Hodder Wayland Picture Library 16 (Gordon Clements), 17, 21 (Jim Holmes), 26 (Gordon Clements), 39 (Paul Kenward).

Graphics and maps: Tim Mayer

Contents

What is Islam?

Islam is the religion of Muslims. Muslims believe in One God, Allah, who created all things. They submit their lives to Allah. This means that they let Allah take charge of their lives and they obey.

Prophets

Muslims believe that, from the beginning of time, Allah sent prophets into the world. The prophets told people how to worship Allah and how to live as Allah wanted. Many of the same prophets are found in three religions: Islam, Judaism and Christianity.

▼ When Muslims pray, they bow down. This shows that they submit their lives to Allah.

Peace and blessings of Allah

Every time that Muslims say the name of the Prophet Muhammad, they add 'the peace and blessings of Allah be upon him'. In writing, the words are shortened to 'pbuh'. In print, this logotype is used:

► This logotype represents the words handwritten in Arabic. Many Muslims speak Arabic.

The Prophet Muhammad

Muslims believe that the final prophet that Allah sent to the world was the Prophet Muhammad. He is called 'the Prophet of Islam'.

They believe that Allah gave his final message for people to the Prophet Muhammad. Later the words were written down to make the Qur'an, the Muslim holy book.

Muslims read the Qur'an to know how to lead good lives, ruled by Allah. The rules of Islam cover every part of life, including eating, drinking and washing.

▼ Family values are important to Muslims.

The Life of Muhammad ﷺ

About 1400 years ago a man called Abd al Muttalib lived in the city of Makkah in Arabia. He worshipped the One God.

Abd al Muttalib's son was married to a woman called Aminah, but he died just before Aminah gave birth to a baby boy. Both Abd al Muttalib and Aminah had a dream that the baby should be called Muhammad ﷺ. This means 'the praised one'.

When Muhammad ﷺ was six, Aminah died and Abd al Muttalib took care of him. Then Abd al Muttalib died too.

Muhammad ﷺ went to work for his uncle as a shepherd and as he grew up, his uncle realized that he could trust him. He gave Muhammad ﷺ a job on his camel trains. This meant that Muhammad ﷺ travelled to different countries.

◀ Muslims never use pictures of the Prophet Muhammad ﷺ. Islamic art consists of patterns and Arabic writing from the Qur'an.

The Ka'bah

The Ka'bah is a cube-shaped building in Makkah which is very important to Muslims. People say that it was built by some of the first Prophets ﷺ as a place to worship the One God. However, later on, people began to worship many gods there. When Muhammad ﷺ was born, there were 360 altars to different gods around the Ka'bah.

When Muhammad ﷺ was 25 years old he went to work for a rich businesswoman called Khadijah, who was 40. She admired Muhammad ﷺ because he was trustworthy and religious and did not drink alcohol. This was different from other men in Makkah.

Khadijah and Muhammad ﷺ were married and had six children: two sons, who died young, and four daughters.

Many people in Makkah did not like having daughters, but Muhammad ﷺ loved his and took them to pray with him.

Words from the One God

Muhammad ⬩ saw that people in Makkah worshipped idols, and made money by selling statues and animals for sacrifice. Many people got drunk and behaved badly. Women were often treated worse than slaves. Muhammad ⬩ knew that the One God, Allah, did not want people to live like this.

One night Muhammad ⬩ was alone in a cave on Mount Hira. The Angel Jibril appeared and told him to read from a roll of silk with letters of fire.

Muhammad ⬩ could not read. He said three times that he could not read out the letters. But suddenly he felt that he knew what the letters said. He began to recite some words. These words are now the 96th *surah* (chapter) of the Qur'an.

The 96th surah

The Qur'an has 114 chapters or sections called *surahs*. Part of the 96th *surah* is:

Recite! In the name of your Lord and Sustainer who created man from a clot of congealed blood, speak those words aloud!

Muhammad ﷺ told Khadijah what had happened. She understood that he was a Prophet of the One God, Allah.

In the next years Muhammad ﷺ received more words from Allah. He began to talk about them. He spoke out against idol worship and the way people lived.

Some people in Makkah agreed with him. Others realized that they would lose money if people stopped buying alcohol and things to sacrifice. Therefore they persecuted the Prophet Muhammad ﷺ and his followers.

One day, the Prophet ﷺ preached to some people from a town called Yathrib. They became Muslims and invited the Prophet Muhammad ﷺ and his followers to live in Yathrib. The Prophet ﷺ believed that Allah wanted him to set up a Muslim state there.

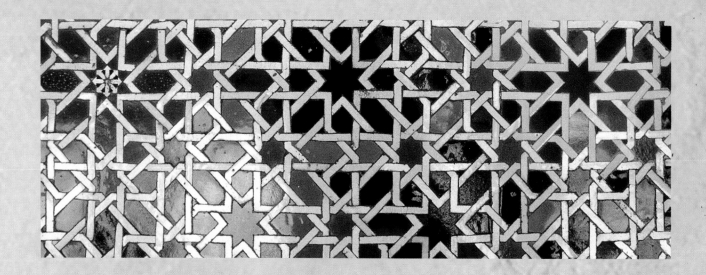

A Muslim state

The Prophet Muhammad ﷺ told his followers to move to Yathrib, to escape persecution in Makkah. Finally he escaped too, with his friend Abu Bakr.

Assassins chased after them, so they hid in a cave. Then a spider spun a web and a bird built a nest over the cave entrance, so the assassins thought there was no one inside. After four days the Prophet ﷺ and Abu Bakr went on to Yathrib. Their journey is known as the *Hijrah*.

The people of Yathrib lined the streets to welcome them. Eventually, the Prophet's ﷺ white camel stopped by a barn. He decided to live and build the first mosque there.

Yathrib became known as Madinah. It was the first Muslim state. The Prophet Muhammad ﷺ led the people according to Allah's laws. Everyone, including the Prophet ﷺ lived simply and centred their lives around Allah. People tried to be equal and servants were well looked after. Women were respected. Jewish people in the city were allowed to practise their own beliefs.

Battles with Makkah

After some Muslims raided a camel train from Makkah, the people of Makkah attacked Madinah. The Prophet Muhammad ﷺ raised an army to fight them and won the battle. More battles followed and the Muslims lost one of them.

Jihad

The Prophet Muhammad ﷺ taught people that Allah accepted war if it was to defend Islam. This is called Holy War or *jihad*. He said that his army must not attack the sick or people who were not fighting. He forbade them to raid houses, to steal, or to destroy fields and farms.

▼ A mosque was built at the centre of Madinah.

The Return to Makkah

About eight years later the Prophet Muhammad ✺ led an army of 10,000 men to Makkah. He rode on his white camel to the Ka'bah (see page 7). Then he dismounted and walked around the Ka'bah seven times. The idols inside were destroyed. At midday the Prophet ✺ called everyone to pray.

The Prophet ✺ and his army had conquered Makkah and only eleven people were killed. The people of Makkah went back to worshipping only the One God, Allah. The Prophet ✺ forgave his enemies and soon everybody in Makkah became Muslims. Non-Muslims were forbidden to enter the city or live there.

A great sermon

The Prophet Muhammad ✺ returned to Madinah, but he made a pilgrimage to Makkah two years later. More than 100,000 people joined him and he preached a great sermon. In it he summarized all the messages that Allah had revealed to him.

◀ This drawing from Persia (present-day Iran) shows the Ka'bah (at the top) and the Prophet's Mosque at Madinah.

The Prophet's ﷺ death

Back in Madinah the Prophet Muhammad ﷺ became ill and died. His last words were, 'Allah, grant me pardon.'

Many of his followers refused to believe that he was dead. His friend Abu Bakr reminded them that the Prophet ﷺ was a human being. He said they must not worship the Prophet ﷺ, but remember him as Allah's last messenger.

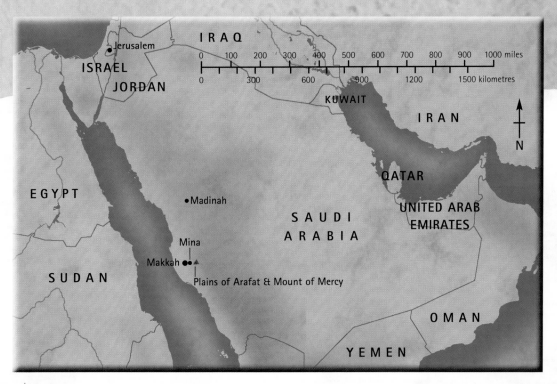

▲ Makkah and Madinah are in present-day Saudi Arabia.

When did the Prophet ﷺ live?

The Prophet Muhammad ﷺ was born in Makkah in 569 CE. He was a member of the most important tribe in the city. He had his first revelation from Allah in the year 610. In 622 he moved from Makkah to Madinah and set up the first Muslim state. He died on 8 June 632 at the age of 63.

The Prophet ﷺ Teaches Allah's message

Muslims believe that the words that the Prophet Muhammad ﷺ spoke came from Allah. So the Prophet ﷺ gave people Allah's message. He was not teaching them his own ideas.

▲ This is the *Shahadah*, written in Arabic. It is on the flag of Saudi Arabia.

Every day Muslims say:

'There is no God except Allah and Muhammad ﷺ is the messenger of Allah.'

This statement of belief is called the *Shahadah*.

Allah

Muslims believe that Allah is greater than any words can really describe. In the Qur'an, 99 names are used to describe the greatness of Allah.

Muslims believe that Allah has no form and cannot be compared to any created thing. Pictures of Allah are forbidden, as are pictures of the Prophets ﷺ. This is so that people cannot worship the pictures. Muslims must worship only Allah.

Prayer

The Prophet Muhammad ﷺ taught Muslims to pray to Allah five times every day. This helps Muslims to put Allah at the centre of their lives. The five prayer times must be part of their daily routine.

Life after death

The Prophet ﷺ taught that there is life after death. After death Allah asks each person about his or her life and decides whether he or she will go to Paradise or Hell. To enter Paradise, people must live good lives centred around Allah.

▲ This poster shows the 99 names used to describe Allah's greatness.

The Five Pillars of Islam

The Prophet Muhammad ﷺ gave Muslims five duties, known as the Five Pillars of Islam. They are:

- To say the *Shahadah*.
- To pray five times a day.
- To fast during the month called *Ramadan*.
- To give part of their wealth to charity.
- To go on pilgrimage to Makkah once in their lifetime, unless they are too ill or too poor to do so.

▲ A Muslim gives aid from Saudi Arabia to Muslims affected by war.

Equal and united

The Prophet Muhammad ۩ said that all Muslims are equal in the eyes of Allah. He also said that all Muslims make up one big community called the *Ummah*.

These ideas of equality and a united community were new. In Arabia in the Prophet's ۩ time, different tribes were always fighting. However, Muslims became united because they had one main belief and one way of life, based on the Five Pillars of Islam (see page 15).

The pilgrimage to Makkah is an important time for showing that all Muslims are equal. All the pilgrims wear white robes, so it is not possible to tell who is rich or poor.

► Around the world Muslims go to their mosque for Friday prayers. They all pray in Arabic.

Money

The Prophet Muhammad ﷺ said that money must not divide Muslims. After paying all their expenses, Muslims must give two-fifths of the money they have left to charity. If they lend money, they must not charge interest.

▼ Muslim women are respected at home and at work. Many women, such as this nurse, have professional jobs.

Women and Islam

Women were not always respected in the time of the Prophet Muhammad ﷺ. But he said:

People, your wives have a certain right over you and you have certain rights over them. Treat them well and be kind to them for they are your partners and committed helpers.

The family

There are records called *Hadith* of what the Prophet Muhammad ☙ said and did. One *Hadith* is:

A man came to the Prophet Muhammad ☙ and asked who should be treated best. The Prophet ☙ replied, 'Your mother'. The man asked 'Then who?' and the Prophet ☙ again replied, 'Your mother.' The man asked again and the Prophet ☙ said, 'Your father'.

Family life is very important in Islam.

Mothers

In the Arab world there is a saying that 'the mother is a school'. This means that children learn about Islam from their mother. At home she sets an example for them and teaches them to pray. She makes sure that they are clean, have good manners and share things.

▼ A mother leads her children in prayers before a meal.

A new baby

When a Muslim baby is born, some words are whispered into the baby's right ear. The words are:

Allah is most great!
Allah is most great!
I testify that there is no God but Allah.
I testify that Muhammad ﷺ is the Messenger of Allah.
Come to prayer
Come to salvation
God is great
There is no God besides Allah.

These words are called the *Adhan*. At mosques they are chanted five times every day, to tell Muslims that it is time to pray.

▲ A father whispers the *Adhan* into his new baby's right ear.

Fathers

The main duty of a father is to provide for his children. He also teaches the children to follow his example outside the home. He helps them to read the Qur'an and takes them to the mosque.

Children and parents

The Prophet Muhammad ﷺ taught that children must respect their parents and look after them in their old age.

Rules for everyday life

The Prophet Muhammad ﷺ gave Muslims rules
and guidelines about everyday tasks. Some of
these rules or guidelines are in the Qur'an.
Others come from the example set by the
Prophet Muhammad ﷺ in his lifetime, as recorded
in the *Hadith* (see page 18).

Keeping clean

There are guidelines in the Qur'an about washing.
Muslims wash in a special way before they say
prayers five times a day. They wash their hands,
mouth, nose, face, arms, head, ears, neck and feet
three times each in clean running water. This
washing before prayers is called *wudu*.

▼ Most mosques
have a place
where people wash
before prayers.

▲ Muslims like to share their food with guests.

▶ Muslims eat with their right hand. This follows the example of the Prophet Muhammad ﷺ.

Food and eating

Muslims must only eat meat that is *halal*. This means that the animal has been killed in a special way that is humane and hygienic. Muslims must not eat meat from a pig or from any animal that has died naturally or been killed in an accident.

At the beginning of a meal Muslims should say '*Bismillah*', which means 'in the name of Allah'. At the end they should say '*al-hamdu-li-Llah*' – 'praise Allah'.

Islamic Law: Shari'ah

In an Islamic country, such as Saudi Arabia, the law is based on the teachings in the Qur'an and the *Hadith*. This Islamic law is called the *Shari'ah* or 'path'.

The Sacred Texts

The Muslim holy book is called the Qur'an. Muslims believe that the words in the Qur'an are Allah's message to all people. The Qur'an tells people how to lead good lives, submitting to the will of Allah.

Beautiful copies of the Qur'an, like this one, show how Muslims love and respect the words.

How was the Qur'an made?

Allah's message was revealed to the Prophet Muhammad ﷺ by the Angel Jibril (see pages 8-9) over a period of 23 years.

Each year in the month of *Ramadan*, the Prophet ﷺ recited everything that he had been told, to make sure that he had remembered it all.

Other Muslims also learned the words by heart. Then, about 18 years after the Prophet Muhammad ﷺ died, his friend Abu Bakr arranged to write everything down exactly as it had been spoken by the Prophet ﷺ.

To make the Qur'an, the writings were put into an order, with the longest section first and shorter sections at the end. Each section begins with 'In the name of Allah'.

▲ Many people use a special stand for reading the Qur'an.

Respect for the Qur'an

The Prophet Muhammad ﷺ probably could not read or write very well, but the words he spoke, which became the Qur'an, are in beautiful Arabic poetry. Muslims believe that the Qur'an is a gift from Allah and they treat it with great respect.

They always wash before touching the Qur'an and they take care not to touch it unnecessarily. They usually place it on a special stool or stand to read it.

Hafiz

Many Muslims today learn the words of the Qur'an by heart, in Arabic. People who know the Qur'an by heart are called *Hafiz*.

Calligraphy

Calligraphy is the art of doing beautiful handwriting. Scribes who copied the Qur'an developed this art.

Muslims are forbidden to use pictures of people or animals to decorate their mosques. Instead, they use verses from the Qur'an, beautifully handwritten in Arabic.

Al-Fatihah

Often calligraphers write the opening section of the Qur'an. This is called *al-Fatihah*. In English it means:

In the name of Allah, Most Gracious, Most Merciful.
Praise be to Allah, Lord of the Worlds,
The Most Gracious, the Most Merciful;
Master of the Day of Judgement.
You alone we worship and
You alone we ask for help.
Guide us on the straight way,
the way of those you have favoured,
Not the path of those who earn your anger, nor of those who go astray.

▼ This man is embroidering words from the Qur'an in gold thread. The cloth he is working on is to cover the building called the Ka'bah (see page 7). A new cloth is made each year.

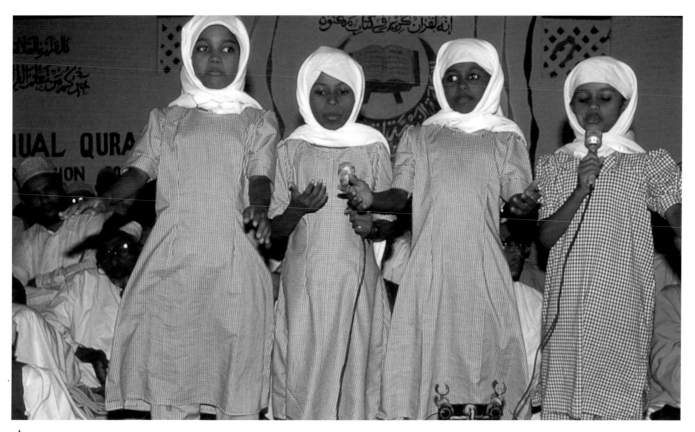

▲ These children in Kenya are taking part in a Qur'an-reciting competition.

Reciting the Qur'an

Muslims everywhere learn to read the Qur'an in Arabic. It is an art to recite the Qur'an. Famous reciters perform the Qur'an at Muslim festivals and there are Qur'an-reciting competitions.

When Muslims recite the Qur'an and tell stories from it, they take great care to recite the words and tell the stories exactly as they are in the Qur'an. Nothing must be changed because they believe the Qur'an is the word of Allah.

The words of Allah

These words about writing come from the Qur'an:

If the ocean became ink for writing the words of Allah, surely the ocean would be dried up before the words of my Lord came to an end.

The Sunnah

Reports of everything that the Prophet Muhammad did and said, together with stories about his life, are called the *Sunnah*. Muslims look at the *Sunnah* as an example of how they should live. One part of the *Sunnah* is the *Hadith*. Another part is the Prophet's biography, called the *Sirah*.

The Hadith

The *Hadith* are sayings about what the Prophet Muhammad said and did. When the sayings were collected, great care was taken to check that they were true and accurate reports about the Prophet When each *Hadith* was written down, the scribe also put a list of the people who had passed on the saying.

▼ These boys are learning to read the Qur'an at a mosque school in Pakistan.

How the Prophet ﷺ cared for animals

Once the Prophet Muhammad ﷺ went to sleep using his only cloak as a blanket. In the morning he found that a cat and her kittens were asleep on his cloak. He cut off the corner they were sleeping on so that they would not be disturbed.

▲ There is little for these calves to graze on but their owner does his best to feed them and care for them.

Muslims believe that the teachings of the *Hadith* come from Allah, but they are not the direct word of Allah like the Qur'an. Therefore Muslims can discuss the *Hadith* in a way that they would not discuss the Qur'an.

One message from the *Hadith* is that people must care for the earth. Allah made people the protectors of the planet and of all living things. Humans must show love and compassion to all living creatures.

The accounts of the Prophet's ﷺ life show that he was kind to animals as well as people.

The Holy Places

Muslims have five main duties (see page 15). One of these is to go on pilgrimage to Makkah at least once in their lifetime. Each year millions of Muslims go on this pilgrimage, which is called the *Hajj*.

Clothes for the Hajj

All the pilgrims wear white clothes called *ihram*. Men wear two white unsewn cloths. Women wear a simple white dress. The clothes are to show the equality and purity of the pilgrims.

The Ka'bah

The first place that the pilgrims go to in Makkah is the Ka'bah, which stands in the middle of the Grand Mosque. Muslims believe that the Ka'bah was built by the Prophets Ibrahim ﷺ and Isma'il ﷺ as a place to worship Allah. Later people

◄ The cube-shaped building called the Ka'bah is covered with a black cloth embroidered in gold.

▲ These pilgrims are on their
way from Makkah to the
Plains of Arafat.

worshipped many idols there, but the Prophet
Muhammad ﷺ changed it back into a place for
worshipping only Allah.

Marwa and Safa

Pilgrims walk around the Ka'bah seven times.
Then they go to run or walk between two hills
called Marwa and Safa. This is to remember how
Hajar, the wife of the Prophet Ibrahim ﷺ, ran
between the two hills searching for water for her
son Isma'il ﷺ. She called for Allah to help her and
the Angel Jibril appeared. The Angel struck the
ground with his wing and a stream gushed forth.
Hajar made the stream into the Well of Zamzam.
After running or walking between the hills,
pilgrims drink from this well.

The Plains of Arafat

Next the pilgrims travel from Makkah to the Plains of Arafat, where the Prophet Muhammad ﷺ preached his last sermon. They spend the day praying.

Mina

After this they go to the town of Mina, where there are three pillars. The pillars represent devils who tempted the Prophet Ibrahim ﷺ to disobey when Allah told him to sacrifice his son, Isma'il. The Prophet Ibrahim ﷺ drove away the devils with stones, and pilgrims remember this by throwing stones at the three pillars. This shows that they reject evil.

▲ Pilgrims on the Mount of Mercy, on the Plains of Arafat.

▼ Throwing stones at a pillar in Mina.

The first Hajj

Muslims believe that it was the Prophet Ibrahim ﷺ who first called people to come as pilgrims to the Ka'bah. Allah commanded him to call people there.

Id-ul-Adha

The *Hajj* ends with the festival of *Id-ul-Adha*, which is celebrated by Muslims around the world. The festival recalls how Ibrahim ﷺ was prepared to sacrifice his son Isma'il ﷺ to obey Allah. Then Allah spared Isma'il ﷺ by putting a ram in his place.

▼ Pictures painted on this house in Egypt show that the inhabitants have been on pilgrimage to Makkah.

Ibrahim ﷺ and Isma'il ﷺ

The Prophet Ibrahim ﷺ believed that Allah had ordered him to sacrifice his son, Isma'il ﷺ. He told Isma'il ﷺ about this and both were ready to obey Allah, even though this meant that Ibrahim ﷺ must kill his son. Isma'il ﷺ was on the altar, ready to be sacrificed, when suddenly Allah sent a ram to take Isma'il's ﷺ place.

Madinah

Madinah (see page 10) is Islam's second holiest city. It is 125 km away from Makkah. Many pilgrims on the *Hajj* also visit Madinah in order to think some more about the Prophet Muhammad ﷺ and the example he set for people.

Madinah today is very different from the simple city where the Prophet ﷺ lived. Beautiful mosques now stand at places connected with him.

The al-Quba mosque stands where the Prophet Muhammad's ﷺ white camel rested and the first mosque was built (see page 10).

The Prophet's Mosque, with its elegant minarets (towers) is built on the site of the Prophet Muhammad's ﷺ simple home. Inside is the

▼ Over time, the Prophet's Mosque at Madinah has become more and more elaborate as different rulers have added to it.

Prophet's ☸tomb and also the tombs of his friends who became leaders of the Muslims after his death.

The Qiblatain mosque is different from all other mosques. When Muslims pray, they face in the direction of the Ka'bah in Makkah. This direction is called the *qibla* and most mosques have an alcove called a *mihrab* to show this direction. However, in the Qiblatain mosque there are two *mihrabs*. One faces towards the Ka'bah and one faces Jerusalem (see page 34).

▲ The Prophet Muhammad's ☸ tomb is in the Prophet's ☸ Mosque at Madinah.

▼ Fatimah's grave is also in Madinah.

Fatimah's grave

The grave of Fatimah, one of the Prophet Muhammad's ☸ daughters, is in Madinah. She died only three months after him, at the age of 30. Fatimah went to many battles with the Prophet Muhammad☸ Many Muslim women try to follow her example as a woman and a mother.

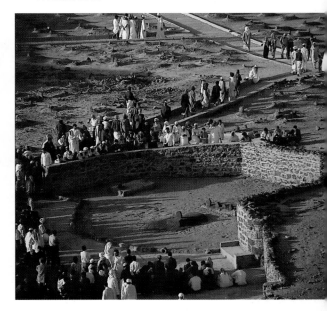

Jerusalem

Jerusalem is the third most holy city in Islam. At first, Muslims faced towards Jerusalem when they prayed. This changed after the Prophet Muhammad ﷺ had a revelation from Allah that people must face the Ka'bah to pray.

Many events in the lives of the Prophets ﷺ took place in Jerusalem. Jerusalem is thought to be the place where the Prophet Ibrahim ﷺ heard Allah's order to sacrifice Isma'il ﷺ. The Prophets Dawud ﷺ (David) and Sulaiman ﷺ (Solomon) built a Temple to the One God in Jerusalem. The Prophet Isa ﷺ (Jesus) preached his message in Jerusalem.

▲ The Dome of the Rock was built where the Temple to the One God had been.

Muhammad's ﷺ footprints

It is said that the Prophet Muhammad ﷺ flew on a winged horse from Makkah to the Temple in Jerusalem. There he climbed a ladder to Heaven and met all the Prophets ﷺ who had gone before him.

After the Prophet Muhammad's ﷺ death, Muslims captured the country around Jerusalem. The Christian ruler of Jerusalem refused to hand over the city unless Umar, the Muslim leader, personally accepted his surrender. Umar went to Jerusalem and found that the Temple had fallen down and was being used as a rubbish dump.

Umar began to clear the site and uncovered some marks in the rock. Muslims believe that these are footprints made by the Prophet Muhammad ﷺ when he climbed the ladder into Heaven. Umar built a wooden mosque there. Later, it was replaced with the Dome of the Rock mosque.

Other religions in Jerusalem

Muslims led by Umar took control of Jerusalem. However, they allowed Jews and Christians in the city to go on practising their own religions. The Muslims realized that Jews and Christians also worshipped the One God.

▼ The rock with the Prophet Muhammad's ﷺ footprints is inside the Dome of the Rock.

Festivals and Family Times

For Muslims, festivals are for praising Allah and remembering the Prophets ﷺ. At festival times, Muslims meet up with family and friends. They also make sure that no one is left on their own for the festival and that poor people have enough food.

Food prepared for a festival.

Al Hijrah

On the Muslim calendar, new year's day is called *Al Hijrah*. It is the anniversary of the *Hijrah*, the Prophet Muhammad's ﷺ move from Makkah to Madinah (see page 10). Muslims celebrate by telling stories about the Prophet ﷺ. They also say extra night-time prayers.

The *Hijrah* was a very important event for Muslims because it was the beginning of the first Muslim state. Therefore on the Muslim calendar the year in which the *Hijrah* took place is called year 1. On the Christian calendar the *Hijrah* took place in AD 622.

The Prophet's 🕌 birthday

The festival to celebrate the birthday of the Prophet Muhammad 🕌 is called *Maulud-an-Nabi*. It is on the twelfth day of *Rabi'ul-Awwal*, the third month of the Muslim year.

Some Muslims do not celebrate this festival as they believe that it is hero worship. But most Muslims do celebrate, with processions, listening to stories about the Prophet Muhammad 🕌 and singing songs about him.

 Muslims in Britain take part in a procession for the Prophet's 🕌 Birthday.

The calendar

The Muslim calendar is based on the moon. Each month begins when a new moon is seen. This makes a Muslim year 11 days shorter than the 365-day year of the more widely used Christian calendar, which is based on the sun. On this calendar, Muslim festivals occur 11 days earlier each year than in the previous one.

In *Ramadan* Muslims fast during daylight. After sunset they break the fast, like these pilgrims at the Prophet's Mosque in Madinah.

Ramadan

The ninth month of the Muslim calendar is called *Ramadan*. It was during *Ramadan* that the Prophet Muhammad 🕌 received Allah's message (see pages 8-9), which became the Qur'an.

Muslims celebrate by fasting on each day of the month, from sunrise to sunset. They feel that fasting brings them closer to Allah and to others. However, young children and people who are travelling or too sick do not have to fast.

During *Ramadan* Muslims also try to read the whole of the Qur'an. One night in the month is called the Night of Power. It marks the very first night when Allah's words were given to the Prophet Muhammad 🕌. On this night of the festival, readings of the Qur'an in mosques go on into the night.

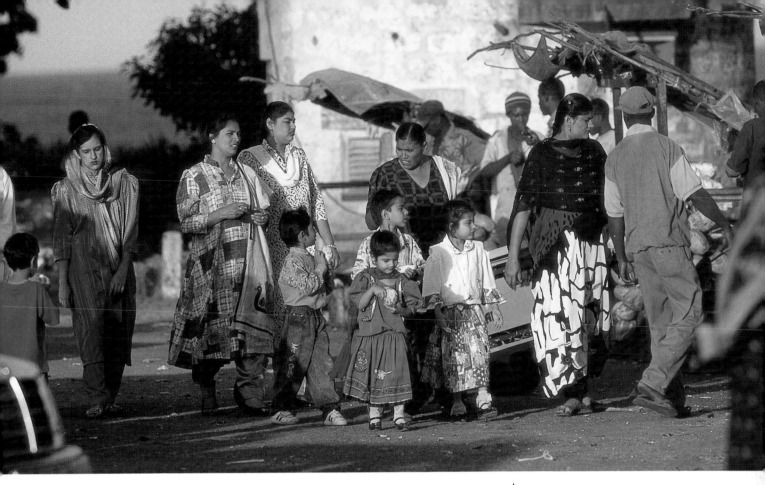

Id-ul-Fitr

Ramadan ends with the festival of *Id-ul-Fitr*. There are prayers. Then presents and cards are exchanged and families and friends get together for feasting. In many countries there are competitions for reciting the Qur'an (see page 25).

Zakat-ul-Fitr

Every Muslim must give money so that their mosque can make sure that everyone has food to celebrate *Id-ul-Fitr*. The money is called *zakat-ul-Fitr*.

Giving for charity (called *zakat*) is one of the Five Pillars of Islam (see page 15). Giving *zakat* reminds Muslims that everything belongs to Allah.

▲ This Muslim family in Kenya put on their best clothes for *Id-ul-Fitr*.

▼ A man gives *zakat* after praying at a mosque.

Id-ul-Adha

Id-ul-Adha is the most important festival in the Muslim year. It takes place in the month called *Dhul Hijjah*, which is the month when Muslims go on the *Hajj* (pilgrimage) to Makkah (see pages 28-31). The festival marks the end of the *Hajj*, but it is celebrated by Muslims all around the world.

Id-ul-Adha means 'the festival of the sacrifice'. It is a time for Muslims to remember the Prophets Ibrahim ☆ and Ism'ail ☆. The Prophet Ibrahim ☆ was willing to carry out Allah's command to sacrifice Isma'il ☆, his son. Isma'il ☆ was willing to be sacrificed, in obedience to Allah. Then Allah sent a ram to be sacrificed instead of Isma'il ☆.

▼ Sheep or goats are usually killed at the festival of *Id-ul-Adha*.

A butcher who kills animals according to Muslim law is called a *halal* butcher.

When they think about this story, Muslims think about their own willingness to give up something that they love to obey Allah.

The Qur'an and the *Hadith* give instructions for celebrating *Id-ul-Adha*. To remember the ram sent by Allah, animals are killed and their meat is eaten. All animals that Muslims use for food must be killed in a special way so that they feel no pain. The meat from an animal is used to feed the family and any leftover meat is given to the poor. In some countries *Id-ul-Adha* is the only time that poor people eat meat.

Halal

Halal means 'permitted'. Muslims only eat *halal* meat. This means meat from any sheep, goat, cow or chicken which has been killed in the permitted way by a *halal* butcher.

▲ This baby's hair has been shaved off at her naming ceremony.

Birth

Muslims believe that a child is a gift from Allah. When a baby is born, the Muslim call to prayer is whispered into its ear (see page 19). One week after the birth there is a naming ceremony.

The most popular name in the world for Muslim boys is Muhammad. For girls, many parents choose Khadijah (the name of the Prophet Muhammad's ﷺ wife) or Fatimah (the name of the Prophet's ﷺ daughter). These people hope that their children will follow the example of the Prophet ﷺ and his family.

A tradition at the naming ceremony is for the baby's hair to be shaved off and weighed. Then the family work out how much that weight of silver or gold would be worth and they give that amount of money to charity. If a child is bald, the parents may still make a donation.

Death

Muslims see death as a time when they can be close to Allah. They try to die in the same way as the Prophet Muhammad ﷺ, who prayed, 'Allah, help me through the hardship and agony of death.' He also asked for forgiveness (see page 13).

Muslim funerals are simple, as Muslims believe that everybody is equal in death. Every Muslim is buried in a shroud made from white cloth. The body is placed in its grave so that it is lying on its right side, facing towards the Ka'bah in Makkah.

▼ Muslims in China visit a graveyard at *Ramadan*.

Islam in the World Today

Every Muslim aims to live a good life, following the example of the Prophet Muhammad ﷺ and keeping Allah's law as written in the Qur'an. Muslim countries aim to be like the first Muslim state which the Prophet ﷺ founded in Madinah (see page 10).

▲ Modern Makkah in Saudi Arabia is very different from the simple place where the Ka'bah was first built.

Yet some people say that it is difficult now to live like the people in Madinah and copy their simple values. The people in Madinah were poor and lived simple lives. In contrast, many Muslim countries today are rich from selling oil.

Ideas about change

Non-Muslims sometimes say that, because the Qur'an was written hundreds of years ago, its laws are out of date. They say that Muslim countries need to update their laws.

Most Muslims would say that this is not the case. The Qur'an shows Allah's way of life. This will always be up-to-date and must never be changed.

They point out that following the laws of the Qur'an has good effects on society. For example, Muslim countries are usually united. There are low crime figures in Muslim countries. In Saudi Arabia, for example, when shop owners go to pray, they leave their shops open and unattended and nothing is stolen.

Compared with this, non-Muslim, Western countries have high crime rates and family values there have been lost. Many Muslims compare Muslim and non-Muslim countries in these ways. They argue that Allah's message, given to the Prophet Muhammad ﷺ, is for all times and all places.

▼ These Muslims are praying in the desert of Wyoming in the USA.

The spread of Islam

After the death of the Prophet Muhammad ﷺ, Islam spread all over the Middle East, Africa, Asia and the Far East. It also spread north into the former USSR and Eastern Europe and then to Britain, Western Europe and the USA. Today, Islam is the fastest-growing religion in the world.

Glossary

Adhan   the Muslim call to prayer. It is chanted before each of the five daily prayer times.

altar   a table where sacrifices are made.

Angel   a messenger from God.

assassin   someone who murders, or tries to murder, a leader.

camel train   a group of camels used to carry goods across the desert.

CE   'in the Common Era'. In societies where people follow several religions, CE is often used in dates instead of AD, which has a Christian origin.

devils   evil spirits.

fast   to go without food.

Hadith   sayings reporting what the Prophet Muhammad ﷺ did and said.

Hafiz   people who know the Qur'an by heart.

Hajj   the pilgrimage to Makkah.

halal   permitted.

Hijrah   the Prophet Muhammad's ﷺ journey from Makkah to Madinah in 622 CE.

holy   kept separate and special, for God.

idol   a statue or picture that is worshipped.

ihram   the white clothing worn by pilgrims on the *Hajj*.

minaret   a tower at a mosque. In many places, the *Adhan* is called from the minaret.

mosque   a building where Muslims pray together.

pilgrimage   a journey made to visit a holy place.

Prophets   people who tell others what God wants. After the names of Prophets other than Muhammad ﷺ, Muslims say 'Peace be upon him'. In this book this has been shown by the logotype explained on page 5.

Qur'an   the Muslim holy book.

Ramadan   the ninth month of the Muslim year. It is in this month that Muslims celebrate how the Prophet Muhammad ﷺ received the Qur'an from Allah.

revelation   something new that is shown or told to someone, especially by God.

sacrifice   to kill an animal or person on an altar, as an offering to a god.

sermon   a speech about how to follow a religion.

Shahadah   the statement that Muslims make about their belief in Allah and the Prophet Muhammad ﷺ.

Sirah   the biography of the Prophet Muhammad ﷺ.

Sunnah   everything that is known about the Prophet Muhammad ﷺ, including the *Hadith* and *Sirah*.

surah   a section or chapter of the Qur'an.

Ummah   the Muslim community, made up of all Muslims everywhere in the world.

wudu   a special way of washing before prayer.

zakat   money that must be given to charity.

Further Information

Books

A Year of Religious Festivals: My Muslim Year by Cath Senker (Hodder Wayland, 2003)

Beliefs and Cultures: Muslim by Richard Tames (Franklin Watts, 1999)

Celebration Stories: A Present for Salima by Kerena Marchant (Hodder Wayland, 2002)

Festival Stories: The Hajj Story by Anita Ganeri (Evans Publishing Group, 2004)

Holy Cities: Jerusalem by Nicola Barber (Evans Publishing Group, 2005)

Holy Cities: Makkah by Rosie Hankin (Evans Publishing Group, 2005)

Islam (Eyewitness) by Philip Wilkinson (Dorling Kindersley, 2005)

Muslim Mosque (Keystones series) by Umar Hegedus (A. and C. Black, 2000)

Religions of the World: Islam by Sue Penney (Heinemann Library, 2003)

Sacred Texts: The Qur'an and Islam by Anita Ganeri (Evans Publishing Group, 2002)

Storyteller: Islamic Stories by Anita Ganeri (Evans Publishing Group, 2000)

The Facts About Islam by Alison Cooper (Hodder Children's, 2004)

Visiting a Mosque by Ruth Nason (Evans Publishing Group, 2005)

World of Festivals: Ramadan and Id-ul-Fitr by Rosalind Kerven (Evans Publishing Group, 1999)

Web pages

http://www.bbc.co.uk/schools/religion/islam

http://www.islam4schools.com

Resources for teachers

http://www.reonline.org.uk
A 'family of websites' including some for teachers and some for pupils. Serves as a gateway to over 300 RE resources drawn from all over the web.

http://re-xs.ucsm.ac.uk
RE Exchange Service (linked to National Grid for Learning) with a 'Teachers' Cupboard' resource page.

http://www.theredirectory.org.uk

BBC Education produces schools media resources on different faiths. See:
http://www.bbc.co.uk/schools

Channel 4 produces schools media resources on different faiths, including *Animated World Faiths.*
Download catalogue from:
http://www.channel4.com/learning

The Islamic Cultural Centre
146 Park Road, London NW8 7RG
Tel: 020 7724 3363

The Islamic Foundation,
Markfield Dawah Centre, Ratby Lane,
Markfield, Leicester LE67 9SY
Tel: 01530 244944
http://www.islamic-foundation.org.uk

The Muslim Educational Trust
130 Stroud Green Road, London N4 3RZ
Tel: 020 7272 8502
http://www.muslim-ed-trust.org.uk

Index